# iPhone Pro Max User Guide

The complete and illustrated Photography and Videography Book to help Beginners and Seniors master their iPhone Camera like a Pro with Camera Tips & Tricks for iOS 15

**BENJAMIN ISRAEL**

Copyright © 2021 BENJAMINISRAEL

All rights reserved. This book is copyright and no part of it may be reproduced, distributed, or transmitted in any form or by any means, including photocopying, recording, or other electronic or mechanical methods, without the prior written permission of the publisher, except in the case of brief quotations embodied in critical reviews and certain other noncommercial uses permitted by copyright law.

Printed in the United States of America

Copyright © 2021 BENJAMINISRAEL

# Contents

INTRODUCTION ..................................................................... 1

CHAPTER ONE: HOW TO SET UP AND GET STARTED WITH YOUR IPHONE 13 PRO MAX ...................................... 3

    know your iPhone 13 Pro Max ........................................ 3

    Turn on and set up your iPhone ..................................... 4

        Preparation for setup .................................................. 4

CHAPTER TWO: IPHONE ....................................................... 7

CAMERA BASICS .................................................................... 7

    How to open Camera on iPhone ..................................... 8

        How to switch between camera modes ............... 9

        How to zoom in or out ............................................. 11

        Take macro photos .................................................. 13

        Take a photo or video .............................................. 13

CHAPTER THREE: HOW TO USE CAMERA TOOLS TO SET UP YOUR SHOT WITH IPHONE CAMERA ............... 15

    Turn the flash on or off .................................................. 15

    Take a photo with a filter ............................................. 16

    Use the timer .................................................................. 16

    Adjust the camera's focus and exposure .................... 17

Use a grid to straighten your shot ........................ 19
How can I apply Photographic Styles to my photos? ........................................................................ 21
    Choose a Photographic Style ........................ 22
How to capture Live Photos using your iPhone camera ............................................................................ 24
How to snap action photos with Burst mode on your iPhone camera ................................................... 25
Learn how you can take a selfie using your iPhone 13 Pro and Pro Max camera ........................... 27
Learn how you can capture photos in Portrait mode ............................................................................... 28
    Take a photo in Portrait mode ............................. 29
    How you can adjust Depth Control in Portrait mode ................................................................................ 31
    How you can adjust Portrait Lighting effects in Portrait mode ............................................................ 32
Learn how you can take Apple ProRAW photos .. 34
    How to Set up Apple ProRAW ............................... 35
    Steps to taking a photo with Apple ProRAW ..... 35
Control the shutter volume on the iPhone camera ............................................................................. 36

How to manipulate HDR camera settings on iPhone .................................................................. 37

    How to turn off automatic HDR ..................... 37

    Turn HDR video off and on .............................. 37

CHAPTER FOUR: HOW TO RECORD VIDEOS WITH YOUR IPHONE CAMERA ....................................................... 39

    How to record a video ....................................... 39

    How to do video recording in Cinematic mode ... 40

    How can I edit my Cinematic videos? ........... 45

        How to turn off the Cinematic effect ............ 46

        How you can change the focus subject in a video recorded in Cinematic mode ............ 47

        How to adjust the dept-of-field in a video recorded in Cinematic mode ......................... 49

    How to transfer Cinematic mode videos from your iPhone to your Mac to edit them in other apps ... 49

    How to record a QuickTake video ................. 50

    Record a slow-motion video ........................... 53

    How to capture a time-lapse video ............... 54

    Change the camera's video recording settings on iPhone ................................................................... 55

    How to adjust Auto FPS settings .................... 55

Turn HDR video off and on .................................................. 56

How you can Turn on/of Lock Camera on iPhone 13 Pro Max .................................................................. 57

CHAPTER FIVE: CAMERA SETTINGS ON YOUR IPHONE ................................................................................................ 58

Save your Camera settings ............................................. 58

Change advanced camera settings on iPhone ...... 59

    Turn Prioritize Faster Shooting off and on ......... 59

    Turn Scene Detection off/on ................................. 60

    Turn Lens Correction off /on .................................. 60

    Turn View Outside the Frame off/on .................... 61

How can I view, share, and print photos on my new iPhone? .................................................................. 61

    How to view your photos on iPhone .................... 62

    How to share and print your photos on iPhone ................................................................................ 62

How can I use the Live Text feature with my iPhone Camera? ........................................................... 62

    Uploading your photos and keeping them up to date across devices ................................................ 65

How do I scan a QR code with my iPhone camera? ........................................................................................ 65

How do I read a QR code using my iPhone camera? ................................................................ 66

How to access the Code Scanner from Control Center .................................................................. 66

CONCLUSION ............................................................... 67

# INTRODUCTION

Everyone on the planet knows that when it comes to photo quality on mobile devices, Apple's iPhone is second to none. With the recent release of its flagships, the iPhone 13 Pro and Pro Max, Apple has even widened this gap with its rivals.

The iPhone 13 Pro Max prides itself with a stunning 6.7-inch Super Retina XDR resolution plus a dynamic refresh rate of up to 120 Hz. It also employs the advanced ProMotion technology and can record video in portrait mode or ProRes, comparable to the ProRAW format, a feature that is still alien to many smartphones.

On the aspect of the processor, the phone brings on board the more efficient A15 Bionic Chip. This is in addition to the Macro Mode designed for close-up shots of small objects.

Then you have the Cinematic Mode which enables you to engage selective focus and do recording in HDR with Dolby Vision. That's not all, you also have the inclusion of outstanding Photo Styles (filters) as well as an enhanced Night Mode feature.

This book provides you all you need to know to optimally use your iPhone 13 Pro Max camera in a step-by-step and easy-to-understand manner.

Whether you're a beginner or an expert, you'll find something useful in this book.

# CHAPTER ONE: HOW TO SET UP AND GET STARTED WITH YOUR IPHONE 13 PRO MAX

## know your iPhone 13 Pro Max

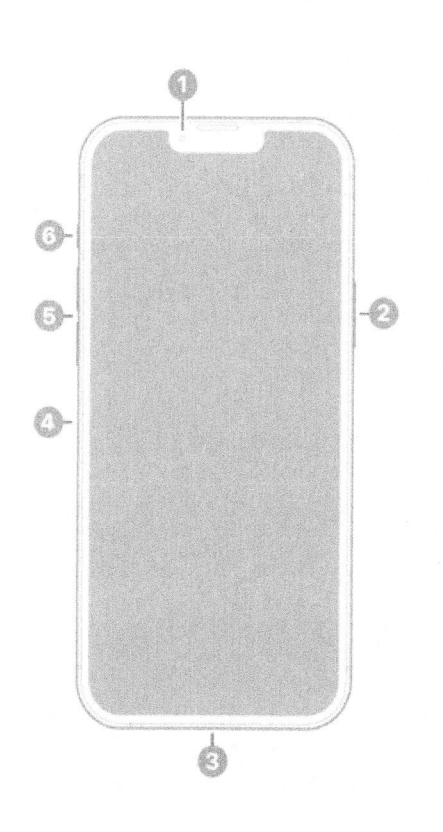

1. Front camera
2. Side button
3. Lightning connector
4. SIM tray
5. Volume buttons
6. Ring/Silent switch

⑦ Rear cameras

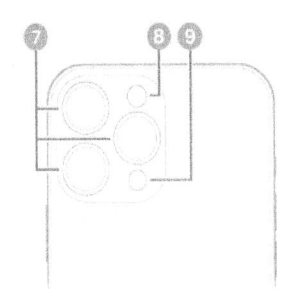

⑧ Flash

⑨ LiDAR Scanner

## Turn on and set up your iPhone

Turn on, as well as, set up your new iPhone using an internet connection. You can also do the set up by connecting your iPhone to your computer. Furthermore, you can safely and seamlessly transfer data from your old iPhone, iPad, iPod touch, or an Android device to your new iPhone.

**NOTE**: If your iPhone is supplied or managed by a company or another organization, see an administrator to guide you through the setup procedures. For general information, you can visit the *Apple at Work website*.

### Preparation for setup

For easy and smooth setup, have the following items handy:

- An internet connection either via a Wi-Fi network or cellular data service through a carrier
- Your Apple ID and password. In case you don't have an Apple ID, you can create one during setup of your device
- Your credit or debit card account information. This is needed if you want to add a card to Apple Pay during setup
- Your previous iPhone or a backup of your device, if you want to transfer data from your old iPhone or device to your new iPhone.

**Tip:** If you don't have enough storage capacity to back up your device, iCloud will grant you as much as you need to complete a temporary backup, for free, but only for up to three weeks from the purchase of your iPhone.

On your previous device, enter into **Settings**, then head to **General**>**Transfer** or **Reset** [*device*]. Click

**Get Started**, and then follow the instructions shown on the screen.

- Your Android device, if you're transferring content from your Android device.

# CHAPTER TWO: IPHONE CAMERA BASICS

One of the greatest achievements of iPhone has been in the area of camera quality. In this chapter, you'll have the chance to learn how operate the Camera of your iPhone 13 Pro Max like a professional. But first, we start with the very basics like how to take photos with Camera 📷 on your iPhone; how to choose from camera modes such as Photo, Video, Cinematic, Pano, and Portrait; and how to zoom in or out to frame your shot.

So, let's get started.

**To use Siri:** You can simply say: "Open Camera."

## How to open Camera on iPhone

You can open your iPhone Camera in the following different ways:

1. By swiping left on the iPhone Lock Screen

2. By tapping the **Camera** icon on the iPhone Home Screen.
3. Locating it in the lower right corner of the Control Center
4. By asking **Siri** to "Open Camera"

**NOTE:** For security purpose, there's usually a green dot showing at the top-right-hand corner of the screen whenever your Camera is in use.

## How to switch between camera modes

Once you open the Camera on your iPhone, the standard mode you'll see is the **Photo**, which is best for taking still and Live Photos. The last photo you captured is usually displayed at the lower left corner, at the center, you have the Shutter button while at the lower right corner, you'll see a circle of arrows which you can use to switch between the main camera and the selfie camera (i.e. the back and front cameras respectively).

You can also swipe left or right to reveal the following camera modes for capturing photos, or video recording:

- *Portrait:* To apply a depth-of-field effect to your photos.
- *Pano:* To capture images wider than the field of view of the camera lens, such as a panoramic landscape or other kind of scene.
- *Square:* To capture photos with a square ratio.

- *Video:* Record a video.
- *Time-lapse:* To capture photos at certain intervals which are then converted to a time-lapse video of motion.
- *Slow-mo:* To record a video with a slow-motion effect.
- *Cinematic:* Apply a depth-of-field effect to your videos, basically a kind of **Portrait mode** for video.

Then you can click ⬆, and click 4:3 to choose between square, 4:3, or 16:9 aspect ratios (also applicable to other iPhone 13 models, iPhone 12 models, iPhone SE (2nd generation), iPhone 11, or iPhone 11 Pro).

## How to zoom in or out

- On all iPhone models, open the **Camera** app and pinch the screen to zoom in or out.
- Just above the menu bar, you'll see the options to toggle between 0.5x, 1x, 2x, 2.5x, and 3x to quickly zoom in or out (based on your model). For a more exact zoom, touch and hold the zoom controls, then move the slider right or left.

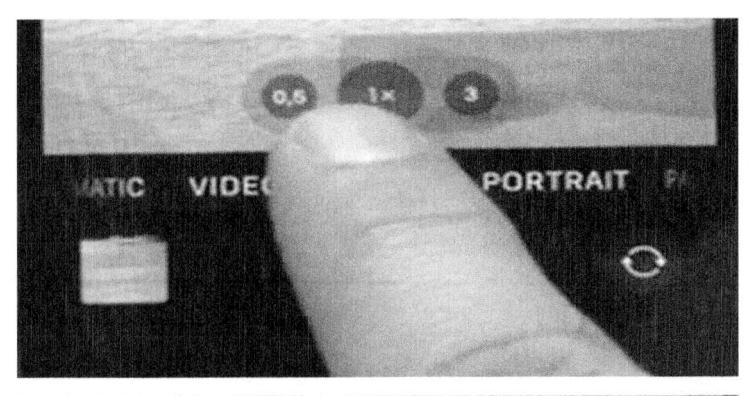

The 1x zoom represents the main camera, and when it is yellow, it means it's active; the 0.5x zoom represents the Ultra-Wide camera while the 3x zoom represents the camera with the telephoto lens.

**NOTE:** The different lenses on your cameras have different technical properties. The main camera, for example, not only produces lesser distortions, but also with the largest aperture, produces quite better results in low-light conditions than the Ultra-Wide camera. The Telephoto lens, on the other hand, with the smallest aperture, produces the worst results in low-light conditions; but also has the least distortions, and is therefore best for taking Portrait photos.

## Take macro photos

The iPhone 13 Pro and iPhone 13 Pro Max have the ability to take macro photos and videos using the Ultra-Wide camera. With this feature, you can capture very minute details of an image by getting very close to it. To take a macro photo or video, launch the **Camera**, then move very close to the subject (about 2 centimeters close) and Camera will automatically stay in focus.

## Take a photo or video

Simply click the Shutter button, or press any of the volume buttons to take a photo.

If you want to take several photos in a roll (or maybe you want to capture that brilliant smile), you can swipe the Shutter button leftwards and hold. This will make your iPhone to take several photos very rapidly in a sequence until you release the button. It's called the **Burst** mode.

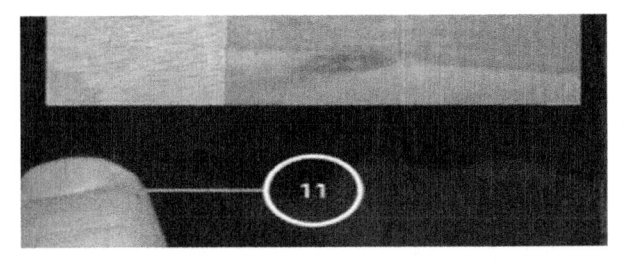

**Tip:** If you like to quickly take a video while in **Photo** mode, touch and hold the Shutter button, and your iPhone will automatically start recording a video. The video stops when you release the button. Apple calls it *"QuickTake video"*. Furthermore, if you want to record a longer video, then click the Sutter button and swipe to the right to lock. Now, your iPhone continues to video even when you release the Shutter button. You'll learn more about that later in the video section below.

# CHAPTER THREE: HOW TO USE CAMERA TOOLS TO SET UP YOUR SHOT WITH IPHONE CAMERA

Before taking a picture, there're available tools on your iPhone camera that you can use to customize and improve your shot. These include turning the flash on or off, setting a timer, adjusting your camera's focus and exposure, straightening your shots with a grid, or even adding a filter.

## Turn the flash on or off

By default, your iPhone camera is set to automatically use the flash whenever the need arises. However, you can manually control the flash before you take a photo, by following these steps:

- *On your iPhone 13 Pro and Pro Max*: Click ⚡ to turn the automatic flash on or off. Click 🔼, then click ⚡ below the frame to choose **Auto**, **On**, or **Off**. You can also follow the same steps if you're using *iP*hone X*S*, iPhone X*R*, and later.

- On iPhone X and earlier: Click ⚡, then choose **Auto**, **On**, or **Off**.

## Take a photo with a filter

Give your photo a befitting color effect using a filter.

1. First of all, select **Photo** or **Portrait** mode, then do one of the following:

   - On your iPhone 13 Pro Max: Click ⌃, then click ⦿.
   - On iPhone XS, iPhone XR, and later: Follow the above step.
   - On iPhone X and earlier: Click ⦿ at the top of the screen.

   Below the viewer, swipe the filters left or right to preview the options; click any one you choose to apply it.

## Use the timer

Use the timer on your iPhone camera to set the time to snap yourself. This is particularly useful when taking a group photo and you want to set the time for iPhone to automatically capture you while putting it on a tripod stand.

- *On your iPhone 13 Pro Max*: Click ⬆, click ⏱, select 3s or 10s, then click the **Shutter** button to start the timer.

- *On iPhone XS, iPhone XR, and later*: Follow the above step.

- *On iPhone X and earlier*: Click ⏱, select 3s or 10s, then click the Shutter button to start the timer.

## Adjust the camera's focus and exposure

Before any photo is captured, the iPhone camera is designed to automatically set the focus and exposure, while face detection sets the exposure at equilibrium across several faces. However, you can manually adjust the focus and exposure by taking the following steps:

1. Click the screen to show the automatic focus area and exposure setting.

2. Click the image, object or person you want to move the focus area.

3. Next to the focus area, you'll see a yellow sun icon ☀, drag it up to brighten or down to darken the exposure of your image.

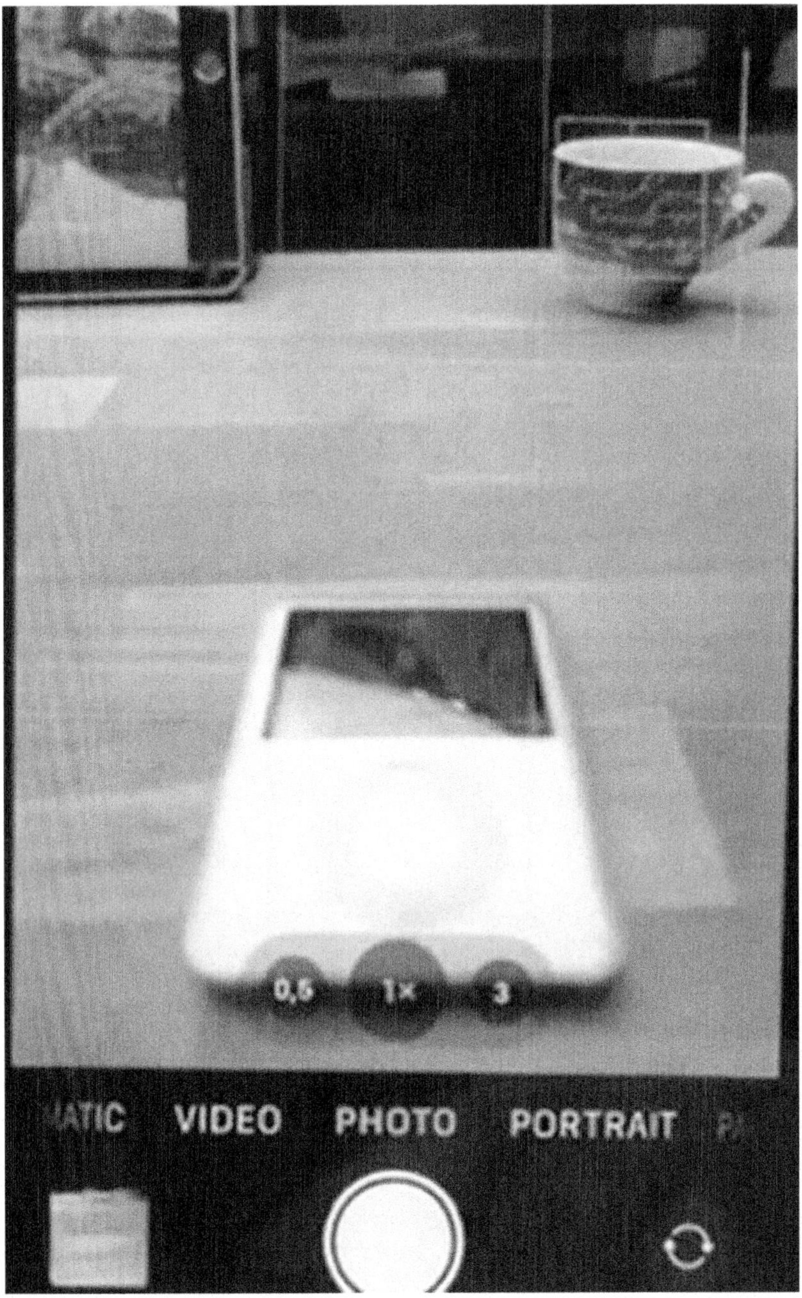

0,5
1×
3
VIDEO
PHOTO
PORTRAIT

To lock your manual focus and exposure settings so that they don't keep changing as you move the iPhone around, touch and hold the focus area until **AE/AF Lock** appears; click the screen to unlock settings.

On your iPhone 13 Pro Max (including iPhone 11 and later), you can exactly set and lock the exposure for upcoming shots. All you have to do is to click ⬆, click ⊕, then move the slider to adjust the exposure. The exposure remains locked until the next time you open Camera. To save the exposure control so that it doesn't reset when next you open Camera, go to **Settings** ⚙, then **Camera**, and proceed to **Preserve Settings**, arrive at **Exposure Adjustment** and turn it on.

## Use a grid to straighten your shot

Displaying a grid on the camera screen can help you straighten and compose your shot. To do this, enter into **Settings** ⚙, go to **Camera**, and turn on **Grid**.

← Settings    **Camera**

Record Slo-mo    1080p at 240 fps →

Record Stereo Sound    ⬤

Preserve Settings    >

Use Volume Up for Burst    ◯

Scan QR Codes    ◯

Live Text    ⬤

**COMPOSITION**

Grid    ⬤

Mirror Front Camera    ◯

View Outside the Frame    ⬤

**PHOTO CAPTURE**

Photographic Styles

Personalise the look of your photos by

After taking a photo, you can add finishing touches to your photo by using the editing tools in the Photos app to further align shots and adjust horizontal and vertical perspective to make you look really professional.

# How can I apply Photographic Styles to my photos?

This feature is available only on iPhone 13 models. Here, you can apply a Photographic Style that'll let you customize how Camera 📷 captures photos. Select from the preset styles, which are: Rich Contrast, Vibrant, Warm, and Cool. Afterwards, you can further customize them by adjusting the tone and warmth values. Camera will apply your choice each time you capture a photo in **Photo** mode. You can change and adjust Photographic Styles as desired right in Camera.

## Choose a Photographic Style

By default, your iPhone **Camera** is set to **Standard** — a well-adjusted style that is true to life. Notwithstanding, you can apply a different Photographic Style, depending on your preference, by following these steps:

1. Open Camera, then click ⌃.
2. Click ⌗, then swipe left to preview the different styles:
   - *Rich Contrast:* This creates darker shadows, with a rich color combination, and stronger contrast to give you a dramatic look.
   - *Vibrant:* Wonderfully bright and vivid colors will give you a brilliant yet natural look.
   - *Warm:* Golden undertones will give you a warmer look.
   - *Cool:* Blue undertones will give you a cooler look.

To customize a Photographic Style, click the Tone and Warmth controls below the frame, then move the slider left or right to adjust the value. Click ↺ to reset the values.

Click ⌗ to apply the Photographic Style you choose.

To change or adjust a Photographic Style that you set, click ⬗ at the top of the screen.

Furthermore, you can change Photographic Styles in Settings: simply go to **Settings** ⚙ > **Camera** > **Photographic Styles**.

# How to capture Live Photos using your iPhone camera

With a Live Photo, you're able to capture what happens just before and after you take your photo, including the audio. You don't really need any extra skill to take a Live Photo than you need to take a normal photo.

1. Launch **Camera** in **Photo** mode.
2. Remember to turn on **Live Photo**. If it's on, you'll see ◉ at the top of your camera. You can turn on Live Photo by clicking ◉.
3. Click the Shutter button to take a Live Photo.

4. To play the Live Photo, click the photo thumbnail at the bottom of the screen, then touch and hold the screen to play it.

NOTE: When **ProRaw** is turned on, Live Photos won't be available.

## How to snap action photos with Burst mode on your iPhone camera

Burst mode on your iPhone camera is designed for capturing a moving subject. It takes multiple high-speed photos so that you have a variety of photos to select from. Burst photos can be taken using the rear and front-facing cameras.

1. On your iPhone 13 Pro Max, swipe the Shutter button to the left to take rapid-fire photos. Apply same procedure if you're using iPhone XS, iPhone XR, and later. On earlier models, touch and hold the Shutter button.

   The counter will display how many shots you've taken.
2. Lift your finger to stop.
3. To select the photos you want to keep, click the Burst thumbnail, then click **Select**.

Gray dots appear under the thumbnails showing the suggested photos to keep.

4. Look down the screen and you'll see a circle in the lower-right corner of the photo you want to keep as a separate photo, click it, and then click **Done**.

To delete the entire Burst, click the thumbnail, then click 🗑.

**TIP:** You can also press and hold the volume up button to take Burst shots. Enter into **Settings** ⚙, go to **Camera**, then turn on **Use Volume Up for Burst** (not available on iPhone models earlier than iPhone XS and iPhone XR).

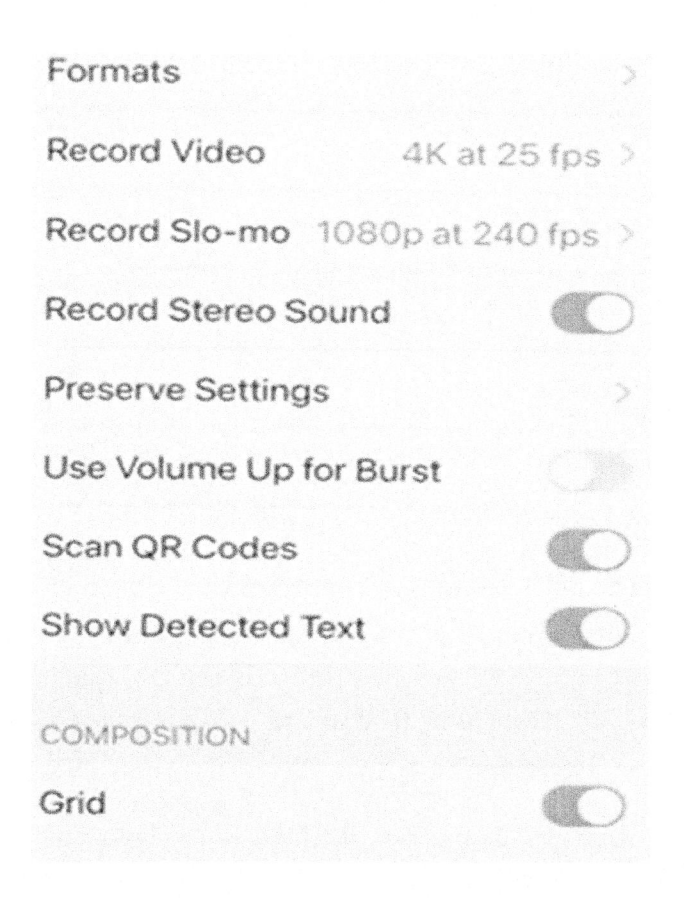

> Formats >
>
> Record Video      4K at 25 fps >
>
> Record Slo-mo  1080p at 240 fps >
>
> Record Stereo Sound          ⦿
>
> Preserve Settings            >
>
> Use Volume Up for Burst      ◯
>
> Scan QR Codes                ⦿
>
> Show Detected Text           ⦿
>
> COMPOSITION
>
> Grid                         ⦿

# Learn how you can take a selfie using your iPhone 13 Pro and Pro Max camera

You can use your front-facing camera to take a selfie in **Photo** mode, **Portrait** mode or record in **Video** mode.

1. Depending on your model, click ⟳ or 📷 to switch to the front-facing camera.
2. Position your iPhone in front of you.

   **TIP:** On iPhone 11 models, iPhone 12 models, and iPhone 13 models, click the arrows inside the frame to increase the field of view.
3. Click the Shutter button or press any of the volume buttons to take the shot or start recording.
4. To capture a mirrored selfie that produces the same image as displayed in the front camera frame, enter into **Settings** ⚙, then head to **Camera > Mirror Front Camera** and turn on the switch.

## Learn how you can capture photos in Portrait mode

With Camera 📷, you can apply a depth-of-field effect to preserve the sharpness of your subject while at the same time create a blurred background. You can even apply and adjust various lighting effects to your Portrait mode photos, as well as take a selfie in Portrait mode as earlier mentioned.

## Take a photo in Portrait mode

You can apply studio-quality lighting effects to your photos in Portrait.

1. Select **Portrait** mode.
2. Follow the tips displayed onscreen to guide you on how you can frame your subject correctly in the yellow portrait box.
3. Drag ⬡ to select a lighting effect:

- *Natural Light:* Makes the background blurred while keeping the face in sharp focus.
- *Studio Light:* Brightens the face and gives the photo has an overall clean look.
- *Contour Light:* Gives the face some dramatic shadows with highlights and lowlights.
- *Stage Light:* The face is spot lit on a deep black background.
- *Stage Light Mono:* Creates a similar effect to Stage Light, but in this case, the photo is in typical black and white.
- *High-Key Light Mono:* Creates a grayscale subject on a white background.

4. Click the Shutter button to capture the shot.

After taking a photo in Portrait mode and you don't like the Portrait mode effect, you can remove it. While in the Photos app , open the photo and click **Edit**, then click **Portrait** to turn on/off the effect.

## How you can adjust Depth Control in Portrait mode

On your iPhone 13 Pro Max (including iPhone XS, iPhone XR, and later), you can use the Depth Control slider to adjust the level of background blur in your Portrait mode photos.

1. Select Portrait mode, then frame your subject.
2. Click *f* in the top-right corner of the screen.

The Depth Control slider displays below the frame.

3. Move the slider to the right or left to adjust the effect. The smaller the values, the stronger the effect would be, meaning a blurrier background; and the bigger the numbers, the less blurred your background becomes, just the way you have it on a bigger camera.
4. Click the Shutter button to take the shot.

The Depth Control slider in Photos is very useful in further adjusting the background blur effect after taking a photo in **Photo** mode.

# How you can adjust Portrait Lighting effects in Portrait mode

If you're using an iPhone XS, iPhone XR, up to the latest model, iPhone allows you to do some adjustments with regards to the position and intensity of the individual Portrait Lighting effect. Such adjustments can do a lot in sharpening eyes or brightening and smoothening facial features. You can do this by swiping to the left or right to reveal the various lighting effects, and then tapping on Portrait Light icon to bring up the slider where you can then make adjustments.

With **Studio Light**, a soft light shines onto the subject, making it well exposed, with **Contour Light**, the external area of the subject is darkened a little, giving the picture a rather more depth and drama look; with **Stage Light**, the image is isolated in the spotlight and the outer surrounding is completely darkened; **Stage Light Mono** produces the same effect, but this time, in black and white; and **High Key Light Mono** instead, lightens the outer area.

1. Select Portrait mode, then move ⬚ to select a lighting effect.

2. Click ⬤ at the top of the screen.

The Portrait Lighting slider will display below the frame.

3. Move the slider to the right or left to adjust the effect.

4. Click the Shutter button to take the shot.

When you finish taking a photo in Portrait mode, you still have the opportunity to carry out further adjustment of the lighting effect by using the Portrait Lighting slider in Photos.

# Learn how you can take Apple ProRAW photos

Using your iPhone 12 Pro, iPhone 12 Pro Max, iPhone 13 Pro, and iPhone 13 Pro Max, you can use Camera ⬤ to capture images/photographs in Apple ProRAW. Apple ProRAW uses the information of a standard RAW format together with iPhone image processing to give you extra creative control when making adjustments to exposure, color, and white balance (not available in versions of iOS earlier than iOS 14.3).

Apple ProRAW is accessible on all cameras, including the front camera. However, it's not supported in Portrait mode.

## How to Set up Apple ProRAW

Enter into **Settings** ⚙, go to **Camera** > **Formats**, and turn on **Apple ProRAW**.

NOTE: Images in Apple ProRAW format contain more information, thereby resulting in larger file sizes.

## Steps to taking a photo with Apple ProRAW

1. Launch the **Camera**, then click ⓡⒶⓌ to turn ProRAW on.
2. Take your shot as desired.

While capturing, you'll have the option to toggle between (RAW) and (R̶A̶W̶) to turn ProRAW on and off.

## Control the shutter volume on the iPhone camera

Use the volume buttons on the side of your iPhone to adjust the shutter volume of the camera. Alternatively, you can swipe down from the top-right corner of the screen while Camera is on, to open the Control Center, and drag down or up 🔊 to either reduce or increase the volume.

If you're the type that likes taking shots without being noticed, you might want to mute the shutter sound completely. Use the Ring/Silent switch on the side of your iPhone to mute the sound. The shutter is silent when Live Photos ◉ is turned on.

**NOTE:** The muting function is disabled in some countries or regions.

# How to manipulate HDR camera settings on iPhone

*HDR* (high dynamic range) in Camera 📷 enables you to get impressive shots in high-contrast situations.

By default, your iPhone automatically use the rear and front cameras to capture photos in HDR when it's most effective. All iPhone 12 and iPhone 13 models do video recording in HDR to capture true-to-life color and contrast.

## How to turn off automatic HDR

As stated above, taking photos in HDR is set by default on your iPhone, especially when that's the most effective means available. However, you can manually control HDR on your iPhone by doing the following:

- Enter into **Settings**, then go to **Camera** and turn off **Smat HDR**. To turn it on again, simply click HDR from your camera screen.

## Turn HDR video off and on

On iPhone 12 models and iPhone 13 models, video recording is done in Dolby Vision HDR for true-to-life color and contrast.

But if you go to **Settings** > **Camera** > **Record Video**, you can turn HDR video recording off.

Now, let's talk more about videos but first, take a little time out to capture a few photos, applying what you've already learnt and we'll see in the next chapter.

# CHAPTER FOUR: HOW TO RECORD VIDEOS WITH YOUR IPHONE CAMERA

Bring the Camera 📷 to record videos on your iPhone and switch to different modes to take slow-motion and time-lapse videos.

**NOTE:** For your privacy, any time the Camera is on, a green dot pops up in the top-right corner of the screen.

## How to record a video

1. Select the Video mode to record in.
2. Click the Record button or press any of the volume buttons to start recording. While recording, you can perform other tasks like:
   - Press the white Shutter button to snap a still photo.
   - Pinch on the screen to either zoom in or zoom out.
   - Touch and hold 1x and move the slider to the left for a more exact zoom.

Click the Record button or press any of the volume buttons to stop recording.

By default, your videos are recorded at 30 frames per second (fps). However, you can choose other frame rates and video resolution settings, which is dependent on the model of your device. Go to **Settings** > **Camera** > **Record Video**. Bear in mind that when you choose faster frame rates and higher resolutions, you're going to have larger video files.

# How to do video recording in Cinematic mode

Cinematic mode is a feature available only in iPhone 13 models. The technology applies a depth-of-field effect that enables you to blur the foreground and background of the subject of your video without losing its sharpness.

What happens is that once in Cinematic Mode, iPhone automatically detects the subject of your video, which could be a person, pet, or object, and brings them into focus throughout the recording. The background and foreground are then blurred around your subject, similar to what you get in Portrait Mode, thereby placing more attention on the subject. This creates a depth-field-effect, a kind of effect used in cinema films.

Once it detects a new subject, it also automatically transitions the point of focus to that subject. You can also manually shift the point of focus while recording, or change it later in the Photos app.

Now, let's do some practical!

1. Open the Camera app on your iPhone 13 model.
2. Swipe anywhere on the screen from left to right twice to select Cinematic mode.

    On iPhone 13 Pro and iPhone 13 Pro Max, you can zoom in by tapping 1x before you start recording.

3. Click the Record button (the red circle) or press any of the volume button to start recording.

    The depth-of-field effect of the Cinematic mode is auto-set. However, you can adjust it if you so desire.

    Click 🅕, then move the slider leftwards or rightwards between 2.0 and 16. before you start recording.

- When you see a yellow frame on the screen, it means the person has been identified as the subject and is in focus; a gray frame means a person is detected, but not in focus. Click the gray box to change the focus; click again to lock the focus on that person.
- If there's no person in the video, click anywhere on the screen to set the focus point.
- Touch and hold the screen and wait for it to lock the focus.

- While in Cinematic Mode, you can do a little swipe up (vertical orientation) or a little swipe leftwards (horizontal orientation) from the middle of your screen to bring up three buttons – a lightning bolt, a +/- icon and an *f* icon.

- Click the lightning bolt to turn on/off your flashlight for extra lighting while recording. The Cinematic mode works best in a well-lit environment.

- The +/- icon allows you to control the exposure, that is, the amount of light the camera takes in, thus enabling you to create a lighter or darker tone in your video

- The *f* icons allows you to adjust the cinematic effect as described above.

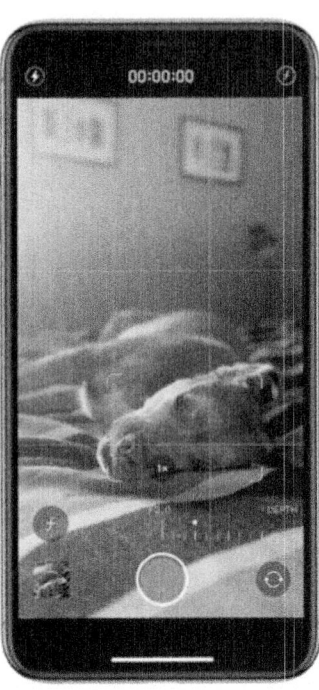

4. Click the Record button or press any of the volume buttons to stop recording.

When you finish recording a video in Cinematic mode, you can remove or change the effect by editing it.

## How can I edit my Cinematic videos?

Although, you can record Cinematic mode videos only on the iPhone 13 series, you can however, edit your Cinematic mode videos on iPhone XS, iPhone XR and later with iOS 15.

## How to turn off the Cinematic effect

1. Launch the **Photos** app, open a video you recorded in Cinematic mode and click **Edit**.
2. Click **Cinematic** at the top of the screen, then click **Done**.

To turn on the Cinematic mode again, repeat the same steps.

## How you can change the focus subject in a video recorded in Cinematic mode

As discussed earlier, once in Cinematic mode, the iPhone camera automatically identifies the subject to bring into focus while you're recording, and as soon as a new object is identified, it also automatically adjusts the focus; but you can decide to manually to do this by doing the following:

1. Launch the **Photos** app, open a Cinematic mode video, then click on **Edit**.

   The white dots you see under the frame viewer show you the Camera automatically changed the focus during recording, while the yellow dots show you where the focus was changed manually.

2. Play the video you want to edit, or just slide the white vertical bar in the frame viewer to the area where you intend to change the focus. A new subject will automatically be identified and outlined in yellow.
3. Click the new subject to change the focus, then click twice to set automatic focus tracking on the new subject. You'll then see a yellow dot under the frame viewer showing that the focus has been changed.
**NOTE:** Another way is to touch and hold the screen and the focus will lock at a particular distance from the camera.
4. Repeat steps 1 – 3 above to change focus points anywhere in the video.
5. To remove a focus you've manually change, click on the yellow dot under the frame viewer, and the click 🗑 .
6. To save your changes, click **Done**.

You can toggle between automatic focus tracking of the Camera and your manually selected focus points by a simple click on ⬚ icon.

After saving your changes, and you don't like your edits, you can still revert to the original Cinematic mode video by clicking **Edit > Revert** when you've opened the video.

## How to adjust the dept-of-field in a video recorded in Cinematic mode

1. Launch the **Photos** app, open a video you recorded in Cinematic mode, and click **Edit**.

2. Click ƒ at the top of the screen. You'll see a slider below the video.

3. Drag the slider leftwards or rightwards to adjust the depth of field effect. Afterwards, click **Done**.

   To cancel any changes made to after you've saved, open the video, click **Edit > Revert**.

## How to transfer Cinematic mode videos from your iPhone to your Mac to edit them in other apps

You can conveniently to transfer Cinematic mode videos from your iPhone to your Mac, using AirDrop, to edit in other apps.

1. Launch the **Photos** app, open the Cinematic mode video, then click ⬆️ .

2. Click **Options** at the top of the screen, and turn on **All Photos Data**, then click **Done**.

3. Click **AirDrop**, then click the device you intend to share with (make sure AirDrop is turned on in the device you're sharing with).

# How to record a QuickTake video

This is the kind of video you record in **Photo** mode. A QuikeTake video can be recorded using your iPhone XS, iPhone XR, and later. When you're doing a QuickTake video recording, you can simultaneously take still photos by simply moving the Record button into the lock position.

1. Got to **Camera** > **Photo mode**, then touch and hold the Shutter button to get your QuickTake video recording started.

2. Slide the Shutter button towards the right-hand side and leave it to lock for a hands-free recording.

- You should see the Record button as well as the Shutter button display below the frame—click the Shutter button to capture a still photo while recording.
- Make an upward swip to zoom in on your subject, or if you're doing hands-free recording, then pinch out on the screen to zoom in.

To stop recording, click the Record button (that's the red circle).

**TIP:** In Photo mode, you can easily start recording a Quicktake video by simply long-pressing any of the volume buttons.

If you click the thumbnail, you'll be able to view the QuickTake videos in the Photos app.

## Record a slow-motion video

When a video is recorded in Slo-mo mode, the video records as normal, you only get to see the slow-motion effect when you play it back. You can make some edits on your video to determine where and when the slow-motion action starts and stops.

1. Open the **Camera** app
2. Select **Slo-mo** mode.
3. Click ⦿ to record in Slo-mo mode with the front camera iPhones 11, 12 & 13 models).
4. Click the Record button (red circle) or press any one of the volume buttons to start the recording.

   If you like to capture a still photo while recording, then click the Shutter button.
5. Click the Record button (red circle) or press any one of the volume buttons to stop the recording.

When you click on **Edit** in the video thumbnail, you'll be able to make some part of the video to play in slow motion and the remaining part play at regular speed. All you need to do is to slide the vertical bars below the frame viewer to enable you determine the section of the video you want to play back in slow motion.

Depending on your device model, you can even change the settings, like frame rate and resolution, for slow-motion recording. To do this, go to **Camera** in **Settings** app , the click **Record Slo-mo**.

**TIP:** You can use quick toggles to chage the video resolution and frame rate while recording.

## How to capture a time-lapse video

This feature enables you to capture footages of events at specific periods of time to make a time-lapse video of an experience over a length of time.

1. Launch the **Camera** app
2. Select **Time-lapse** mode.
3. Set up your iPhone where you want to capture a scene in motion.
4. Click the Record button to start recording; click it again to stop recording.

**Tip:** On your iPhone device, not earlier than iPhone 12 models, use a tripod to capture time-lapse videos with more quality when recording in poorly lit environments.

# Change the camera's video recording settings on iPhone

By default, your iPhone is designed to record videos at 30 frames per second (fps). However, newer models of iPhones come with the options to select other frame rates and video resolution settings according to your preferences. The issue though, is that, when you choose faster frame rates and higher resolutions, your video files are definitely going to be larger in size, and consequently, take up more memory space.

Earlier, I showed you a tip on how you can also use quick toggles to easily change video resolution and frame rates right on the camera screen.

**How to adjust Auto FPS settings**

If you use iPhone XS, iPhone XR, and later, your iPhone is able to enhance the video quality in low-light conditions by automatically lowering the frame rate from the default 30 fps to 24 fps.

To change this, enter into **Settings** , go to **Camera,** and head to **Record Video**, then do one of the following:

- *On iPhone 12 models and later*: Click **Auto FPS**, then apply Auto FPS to only 30-fps video or to both 30- and 60-fps video.
- *On iPhone XS, iPhone XR, iPhone SE (2nd generation), and iPhone 11 models*: Turn **Auto Low Light FPS** on.

**Turn HDR video off and on**

If you're using iPhones 12 and 13 models record video in HDR and share them with devices using iOS 13.4, iPadOS 13.4, macOS 10.15.4, or later; unsupported devices receive an SDR version of the same video. To turn off HDR recording in your iPhone, enter **Settings** > **Camera** > **Record Video**, then turn off **HDR Video**.

**How you can Turn on/of Lock Camera on iPhone 13 Pro Max**

The Lock Camera feature (available only on iPhone 13 Pro and iPhone 13 Pro Max), helps to prevent automatic switching between cameras in the process of recording a video. Lock Camera is off by default but you can turn it on in **Settings** > **Camera** > **Record Video** > **Lock Camera**.

# CHAPTER FIVE: CAMERA SETTINGS ON YOUR IPHONE

## Save your Camera settings

You can save the camera mode, filter, lighting, depth, and Live Photo settings you used last to save you the stress of having to set them every time you need to use the Camera.

1. Head to Settings > Camera > Preserve Settings.
2. Turn any of the following on depending on what you like:
   - *Camera Mode:* Save the last camera mode you used, such as Cinematic or Portrait.
   - *Creative Controls:* Save the last settings you used for the filter, lighting option (on iPhone 8 Plus, iPhone X, and later), or depth control (on iPhone XS, iPhone XR, and later).
   - *Exposure Adjustment:* Save the exposure control setting (on iPhone 11 and later).
   - *Night mode:* Save the Night mode setting instead of allowing it to reset to Auto (on iPhone 12 and later).

- *Portrait Zoom:* Save your last Portrait mode zoom so it doesn't have to reset to the default lens (on iPhone 11 Pro, iPhone 11 Pro Max, iPhone 12 Pro, iPhone 12 Pro Max, iPhone 13 Pro, and iPhone 13 Pro Max).
- *Apple ProRAW:* Save the Apple ProRAW setting (on iPhone 12 Pro, iPhone 12 Pro Max, iPhone 13 Pro, and iPhone 13 Pro Max).
- *Live Photo:* Save the Live Photo setting.

## Change advanced camera settings on iPhone

Get to know more about advanced iPhone camera features that allow you capture photos more quickly, apply personalized and improved looks to your photos, and view content outside the camera frame.

### Turn Prioritize Faster Shooting off and on

On your iPhone XS, iPhone XR, and later models, the **Prioritize Faster Shooting** setting modifies how images are processed—allowing you to capture more photos when you rapidly click the Shutter button

By default, the Prioritize Faster Shooting is turned on, but you can turn it off in **Settings** ⚙ > **Camera** > **Prioritize Faster Shooting**.

## Turn Scene Detection off/on

On iPhone 12 models and iPhone 13 models, the **Scene Detection** setting is able to identify what you're taking a photo of and apply a customized look to reveal the best qualities in the scene.

Scene Detection is on by default, but you can turn it off by going to **Settings** ⚙ > **Camera** > **Scene Detection**.

## Turn Lens Correction off/on

On iPhone 12 models and iPhone 13 models, the **Lens Correction** setting adjusts the photos you capture with the front camera or Ultra Wide camera to give a more natural-looking result.

Lens Correction is on by default, but you can turn it off by going to **Settings** ⚙ > **Camera** > **Lens Correction**.

## Turn View Outside the Frame off/on

On iPhone 11 models, iPhone 12 models, and iPhone 13 models, the camera preview shows content outside the frame to let you know what you can also capture by using another lens in the camera system that has a wider field of view. To turn off this display, enter **Settings** , go to **Camera**, then turn off **View Outside the Frame**.

# How can I view, share, and print photos on my new iPhone?

All the photos and videos you take with your iPhone Camera are saved in Photos. If you turn on iCloud Photos, all new photos and videos will be automatically uploaded and available in Photos on all your devices if they are also set up with iCloud Photos (including iOS 8.1, iPadOS 13, or later).

**NOTE:** When you turn on **Location Services** in Settings > Privacy, photos and videos are labeled with location data. This data can be used by apps and photo-sharing websites.

## How to view your photos on iPhone

1. When you open the **Camera** app, click the thumbnail image in the lower-left corner.
2. Swipe left or right to see the photos you've taken recently.
3. Click the screen to show or hide the controls.
4. Click All Photos to see all your photos and videos saved in Photos.

## How to share and print your photos on iPhone

1. While viewing a photo, click ⬆️.
2. Choose an option such as AirDrop, Mail, or Messages that you want to use share you photo.
3. If you rather like to print your photo, then swipe up to select Print from the list of actions.

# How can I use the Live Text feature with my iPhone Camera?

With your iPhone's Camera app 📷, you can simply copy and share text; you can also open any website address, compose an email, and make a phone call by using the text from your camera frame.

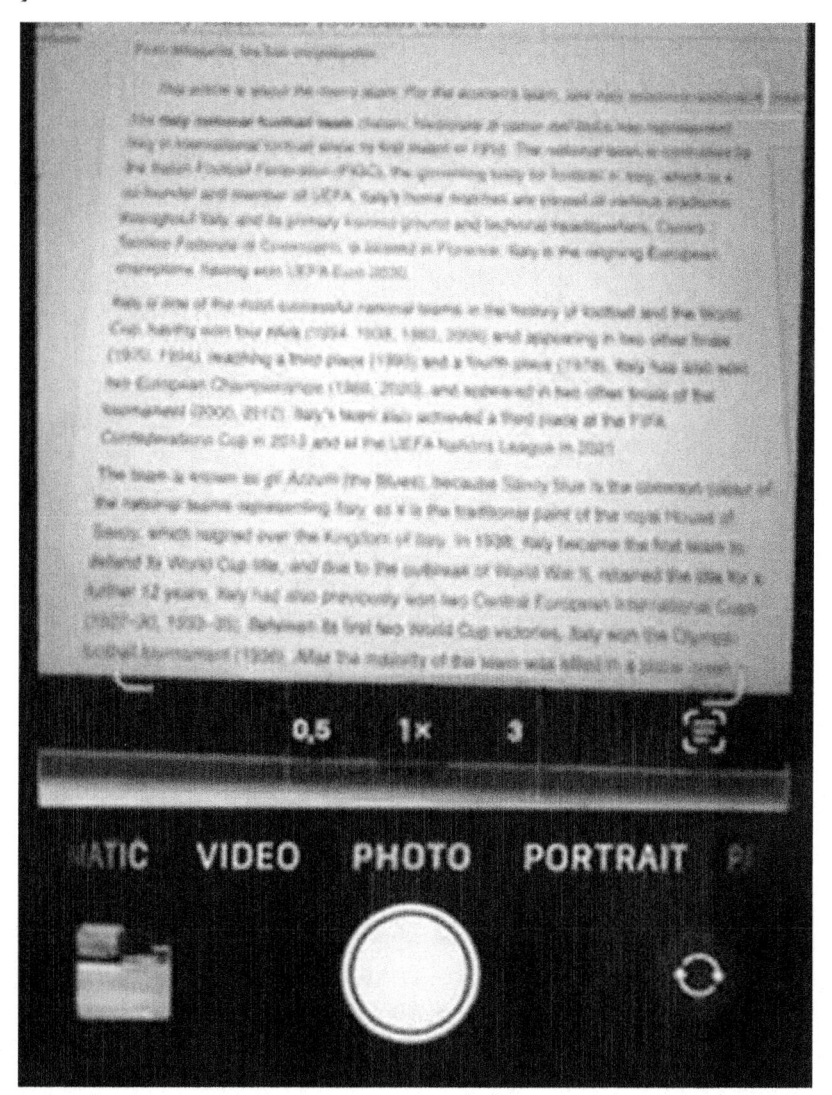

1. Open the **Camera** and position your iPhone in a way that the text appears within the camera frame.
2. Wait for a yellow frame to appear around detected text, then click the text icon at the lower right corner.
3. Swipe or drag the grab points to pick out text. Once you've chosen the text, you can take any of the following further actions:
    - *Copy Text:* Enables you to copy and paste text into a different app, for example, Notes or Messages.
    - *Select All:* Use this to pick out all the text inside the frame.
    - *Look Up:* Used to search text on the net.
    - *Translate:* Used for translating text.
    - *Share:* Used for sharing your text with others using AirDrop, Messages, Mail, or any other options available, depending on your device model.

Click the website address, phone number, or email address captured on the screen and you'll be able to open the respective website, make a call to the number or send an email.

Click ![icon] to go back to Camera.

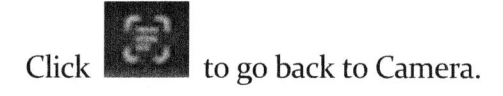

## Uploading your photos and keeping them up to date across devices

Use iCloud Photos to keep your photos and videos up to date on all your devices and save storage space on your iPhone by uploading them to iCloud. You can thereafter access them anytime you sign in with your Apple ID on other devices.

Enter **Settings** ![icon] > **Photos** and turn on iCloud Photos.

## How do I scan a QR code with my iPhone camera?

Use your iPhone's **Camera** ![icon] or the **Code Scanner** to scan Quick Response (QR) codes to get links to open websites, apps, coupons, tickets, etc. The camera is going to automatically detect and pick a QR code.

## How do I read a QR code using my iPhone camera?

1. Open the Camera app, then place your iPhone in the position that lets the code appear on the screen.
2. Click on the notification that displays on the screen. It'll take you to the relevant website or app.

## How to access the Code Scanner from Control Center

1. Enter **Settings** > **Control Center**, then click close to Code Scanner.
2. Open **Control Center**, click the **Code Scanner**, then position your iPhone in a way that lets the code appear on the screen.
3. To add more light, turn on the flashlight by tapping on it.

# CONCLUSION

Thank you for buying a copy of this book, I hope you found it useful. This book is the second part of the Book Series, "Apple *iPhone 13 Pro Max User Manual for Men and Women*".

If you want to know more about the iPhone 13 series and how you can use your iPhone to the fullest, I encourage you to check the other books in this series to find more useful contents not covered in this book.

You may also want to order for the complete series of books as one compilation (All-in-One) covering the a – z of all you need to know about your iPhone 13 Pro Max from the Amazon store.

You're well appreciated.

Enjoy using your device!